A Wounded Mother

AN INWARD JOURNEY OF LOVING SELF

YESENIA FERNÁNDEZ WALDRON

A Wounded Mother

An Inward Journey of Loving Self

Yesenia Fernández Waldron

Title: *A Wounded Mother: An Inward Journey of Loving Self*
Author: *Yesenia Fernández Waldron*

Publication Date: May 11th 2025 (Mother's Day)

Available Formats: Ebook & Paperback

ISBN:

978-1-964313-14-6 (e-book)

978-1-964313-15-3 (Paperback-book)

About Lost Raven Studios

Lost Raven Studios is dedicated to publishing works that explore the intersection of spirituality, psychology, and personal growth. Our mission is to provide readers with transformative insights and practical guidance for navigating life's complexities and discovering deeper meaning. Through innovative storytelling and deep spiritual wisdom, Lost Raven Studios invites readers to embark on journeys of Self-discovery and healing.

Contact Information:

Website: Lost Raven Studios.com

Email: LostRavenStudios@Gmail.com

Meet The Author

I am Yesenia Fernández Waldron, an artist, a mother, and a woman of color (WOC) on a journey of healing. Born and raised in NYC, my Dominican roots and Capricorn/Cancer spirit have shaped me into someone who moves through life with both resilience and deep introspection. As a mother of three—including my spouse, Dr. Aaron Waldron—I have come to understand the complexities of love, sacrifice, and transformation. My path has been shaped by religious & childhood trauma, a series of complicated wounds that run deep, but one that has also fueled my passion to help WOC reclaim their feminine power. My work centers on the Wounded Mother archetype, exploring how trauma—especially religious & childhood trauma—has impacted the way WOC experience motherhood, identity, and healing. As I pursue becoming a licensed clinical mental health counselor, I am committed to creating spaces where WOC can rediscover themselves in a intergenerational way; beyond the pain, beyond the expectations, and beyond the narratives that have kept them small. This is not just my work—it is my life's calling. Healing is not a destination; it is a journey, and I walk it with those who are ready to reclaim their power and step into their wholeness.

Acknowledgments

This book emerged from the depths of my own becoming—a descent I could not have made alone.

To my mother, thank you for giving me life, and for doing your best with the tools you were given. I honor you. I have come to understand your silences, your strength, and your wounds in a new light. This book is part of my healing and, I hope, part of yours too. You taught me resilience, even in your breaking, and I carry your legacy with tenderness and reverence. You have been both a mirror and a teacher, showing me not only who I am but also who I strive to become. Whether through love or lessons, you have been an undeniable force in my becoming, and for that, I am grateful.

To the mothers who came before us—my grandmothers, whose names I speak in meditation and silence—you carried what could not be spoken and passed down what your hands could hold. Your stories, both told and buried, are the ground from which I rise.

To my children, thank you for being my mirror, my teacher, and my guide. You cracked me open in the most sacred way, and through you, I learned to mother myself.

To my partner in life—your patience, quiet strength, and unwavering presence gave me the space to fall apart and find myself again.

To the sisterhood of women—those I know and those I've never met—who dared to speak the truth of their pain, rage, tenderness, and resilience: your voices echoed in mine when I thought I had none.

To the thinkers, mystics, therapists, and rebels whose words lit the path when mine were still forming—thank you for giving language to the sacred terrain of the psyche.

And to the Divine Feminine in all her names and faces—Sophia, Black Madonna, Mother Earth—you held me when I felt most alone. You whispered wholeness into the dark.

Finally, to the wounded mother in me—thank you for not turning away. Thank you for choosing love.

CONTENTS

CHAPTER 12

CHAPTER 13

CHAPTER 14

Introduction

The grief of a mother like Demeter, the Greek Goddess of harvest, when she searched for her abducted daughter Persephone, echoes across millennia. Persephone was abducted by Hades, the god of the underworld, who desired her as his queen. A man taking what he wants, to include a woman (nothing new). He took her to the underworld without Demeter's knowledge. Imagine hearing a primal scream of maternal grief that brings chills to your skin. A sound of anger and power that resonates with most if not every woman. This ancient Greek myth, where a mother's sorrow plunges the world into barren winter, serves as a mournful illustration of the Wounded Mother archetype—a figure whose pain and vulnerability are as profound as her nurturing power. This archetype, as illuminated by the late Swiss Psychologist, Carl Jung, resides within the landscape of our collective unconscious, populated by universal, inborn patterns and images. These archetypes, foundational to our understanding of human experience, act as organizing principles, shaping our perceptions and interactions with the world. Among these, the mother archetype stands as a potent and complex figure, embodying not only our personal mothers but also a broader entanglement of maternal solicitude, nurturing wisdom, and the very essence of feminine authority.

As I reflect on my own journey through grief, healing, and inner transformation, I often find myself returning to the story of Demeter—not as a distant myth, but as a mirror. Demeter's story has become more than just an agricultural allegory to me. It is an emotional and spiritual roadmap, charting the raw terrain of a mother's grief and the sacred archetypal journey through descent, rupture, and eventual transformation. I have come to understand this myth not just as a tale from the past, but as a sacred reflection of what it means to hold maternal energy—whether toward a child, a community, or my own inner being. When Demeter loses her daughter Persephone to the underworld, I feel that loss in my bones. Her grief isn't passive; it's fierce, volcanic, consuming. She withdraws life from the earth itself, and I recognize that kind of grief—that ache that swallows the ability to nurture. There have been times when I, too, have withdrawn from life, from creativity, from connection, because the pain was too deep to bear. This sacred descent into sorrow is something I know intimately. It is the same spiritual descent that comes when past trauma resurfaces or when my inner child cries out for care. It is the unraveling that happens when I confront my limitations as a caregiver, and must face the quiet, buried wounds that still live in me.

Demeter's withdrawal from the earth is so profound that the seasons themselves are halted. I have felt that, too—my emotional landscape turning barren, frozen. When maternal wounds go unacknowledged, they become echoes that touch everything. The world around me mirrored my inner drought, my silence, my numbness. In those moments, I wasn't able to pour life into others because I hadn't yet given myself permission to grieve. That inner collapse—like Demeter's barren earth—was not the end of the story, but a sacred pause. A call inward. And just as Persephone returns each spring, I began to return to myself. But I wasn't the same. And neither was she. Her return was not a reversal, but a ritual—a new way of holding the rhythm of presence and absence. Through intentional practices, through quiet acts of reconnection, I learned how to mother myself. I created altars to healing. I wrote letters to the little girl in me who had longed for love. I began to embrace the truth that the wound doesn't always go away, but it can become a wellspring of wisdom. The more I embraced these cycles, the more I found peace in their impermanence.

Persephone's descent became a powerful symbol of shadow integration for me. She didn't just survive the underworld—she became Queen of it. That taught me something profound: that the inner child I once thought was fragile was actually a source of power. She had learned to hold both light and darkness. She carried the medicine of the underworld—of trauma, of silence, of sorrow—and now she teaches me how to listen, how to guide others from that place of knowing. I no longer see the dark as something to escape, but as a realm that can be honored and navigated with courage. The meta-spiritual meaning of this myth continues to unfold for me. Demeter's healing isn't linear, and neither is mine. What she gains is not closure, but a deeper wholeness. She becomes a mother who knows the rhythms of gain and loss, death and rebirth, presence and absence. That, to me, is the gift of the Wounded Mother archetype. It reminds me that grief can be holy. That sorrow is not failure. That nurturing—whether it is of another, of a community, or of my own self—begins with the sacred mourning of what was once lost. In this, I find grace. I find a home in the cycles. And I find strength in knowing that healing is not about returning to who I was, but becoming who I am now—more whole, more wise, and more able to love from the depth of what I've survived.

The mother archetype, while often associated with nurturing and life-giving qualities, is not devoid of shadow. Jung recognized its inherent ambivalence, acknowledging a "negative side" that encompasses the hidden, the dark, the devouring, and the terrifying. This duality, encapsulated in the concept of the "loving and the terrible mother," highlights the multifaceted nature of the archetype. When our personal experiences with our mothers, or our projections onto the archetype, are fraught with difficulty, they can give rise to what Jung termed a "mother-complex," invariably intertwined with the notion of injury and illness. It is within this framework that the Wounded

Mother archetype emerges, acknowledging the potential for pain, difficulty, and even trauma that permeates the maternal experience, both for the mother herself and for those who relate to her. This wound, a culmination of personal histories, societal pressures, and the weight of unrealistic expectations, underscores the vulnerability inherent in the maternal role. Yet, within this acknowledgment of woundedness lies the potential for profound healing. The Wounded Mother archetype, echoing the concept of the "wounded healer," suggests that our own wounds can become a source of understanding and healing for others. By confronting and engaging with the imperfections and challenges inherent in motherhood and the feminine in general, we embark on a journey of transformation.

This Journey Entails

Developing Empathy and Compassion: Recognizing the potential for wounding within the mother figure, both personal and archetypal, fosters a deeper compassion towards ourselves and others.

Integrating the "Shadow": Acknowledging the "terrible" aspects of the mother archetype facilitates the integration of our personal "shadow," the disowned parts of ourselves, crucial for achieving psychological wholeness.

Reorienting Values: Engaging with the mother archetype, particularly in the context of motherhood, necessitates a reorientation of values as we confront new realities and responsibilities.

Embracing Ambiguity and Differences: Recognizing the multifaceted nature of the mother archetype, with its interplay of light and dark, cultivates a "tolerance for contradictions, a tolerance for ambiguity." This resonates with Gloria Anzaldúa's concept of la conciencia de la mestiza, which champions the ability to sustain contradictions and transform ambivalence into creative potential. [1]

The Wounded Mother archetype proposes that true healing and a genuine embrace of diversity stem not from an idealized vision of motherhood or the feminine, but from acknowledging and integrating the full spectrum of experiences, including the pain and the potential for growth that arise from our relationship with this powerful archetype. This approach allows us to transcend simplistic dualities and cultivate a more holistic and accepting understanding of ourselves and others. A Wounded Mother is a person whose experience of motherhood—whether literal, symbolic, or spiritual—is shaped by unresolved emotional, psychological, or spiritual wounds that challenge their capacity to nurture, connect, and hold space, both for others and for themselves. While often used to describe individuals in a caregiving or parental role, the Wounded Mother also points to an archetypal journey that transcends biology, gender, or societal roles, speaking to the universal struggle of tending to one's own inner pain while attempting to offer care.

On the psychological level, these wounds may originate from being raised in environments of emotional neglect, abuse, criticism, or abandonment. They manifest as difficulties with self-care, emotional regulation, boundary-setting, and the ability to form secure, empathic relationships. The person may carry an internalized negative maternal voice, experience feelings of shame or unworthiness, or unconsciously project disowned parts of themselves—the "shadow"—onto others, particularly those they are attempting to nurture.

---

1 See Gloria Anzaldúa, Borderlands / La Frontera : The New Mestiza (San Francisco: Aunt Lute Books, 1999).

On the meta-spiritual level, the Wounded Mother is not only a parent to others but a mother to the Self. This involves the sacred and often painful task of re-parenting the inner child—that vulnerable, imaginative, wounded part of the psyche that longs for love, safety, and acceptance. The Wounded Mother archetype calls us inward, to the soft and fertile terrain of our own suffering, asking us to extend compassion where there was once survival, to offer presence where there was once absence.

This archetype also embodies the feminine dimension of the Wounded Healer—one who heals not by erasing pain but by honoring it as sacred wisdom. The feminine energy expressed here is not confined to gender; it is a spiritual frequency characterized by intuition, receptivity, emotional depth, and the power to create space for transformation. In this light, the Wounded Mother becomes a vessel of healing not because of their perfection, but because of their willingness to embrace their imperfections as a sacred path. The descent into the Wounded Mother is often initiated by crisis—loss, motherhood, trauma, or spiritual awakening—that strips away illusions of control and opens the self to deeper truths. This descent can feel like falling into a dark well, where identity dissolves and the soul confronts its rawest wounds. But within that darkness lies the possibility of rebirth—a new kind of nurturing that arises not from obligation or idealism, but from embodied wisdom, integration, and inner authority. The Wounded Mother is not a broken identity, but a living process. It is the work of becoming whole through the radical act of self-compassion and the reclamation of one's voice, body, and truth. Whether showing up for a child, a community, or the Self, the Wounded Mother reminds us that healing often emerges not in spite of the wound, but through it—and that the deepest love grows from the soil of our own becoming.
In "A Wounded Mother," the exploration of the Wounded

Mother archetype serves as a profound journey of self-healing, both universal and intimately personal. This introductory chapter sets out to delve into the multifaceted dimensions of this archetype, aiming to uncover its significance in contemporary spiritual and psychological contexts. Central to this exploration is the recognition of how the Wounded Mother archetype intersects with cultural, social, and ancestral realms, particularly from the perspective of Women of Color. This intersectionality enriches the narrative, offering a nuanced understanding of how various dimensions of identity shape and inform the experience of the wounded feminine.

Purpose and Scope

The primary purpose of this book is to illuminate the transformative potential inherent within the archetype of the Wounded Mother. By examining this archetype through a lens that integrates spirituality, psychology, and cultural studies, this book seeks to offer pathways and perspectives for healing and empowerment. I aim to guide readers on a journey of self-discovery and healing, providing tools and insights drawn from both academic scholarship and personal narratives. The scope of the exploration encompasses not only theoretical frameworks but also practical applications, inviting readers to engage deeply with their own experiences and perceptions of the wounded feminine.

A Woman of Color's Perspective

Central to this exploration is the perspective of Women of Color, whose experiences of the Wounded Mother archetype are intricately entangled with intersections of race, ethnicity, culture, and social justice. By foregrounding these perspectives, this book aims to amplify voices often marginalized in discussions of archetypal psychology and spirituality. It highlights how the wounded feminine manifests uniquely within diverse cultural contexts, offering profound insights into resilience, identity, and community healing. This interdisciplinary approach underscores my commitment to inclusivity and social relevance in its exploration of universal themes through diverse lenses.

Definitions and Inspirations

Introducing the archetypal framework of a Wounded Mother, this book draws inspiration from an intersection of thinkers and theorists. Influences range from Carl G. Jung's seminal work on archetypes to Henri Nouwen's contemplations on spiritual woundedness. Additionally, the contributions of scholars such as Lisa Marchiano, Ada María Isasi-Díaz, Gloria Anzaldúa, and Christena Clevland offer perspectives grounded in Feminist theology, Womanist theology, Mujerista theology and cultural criticism. This interdisciplinary approach not only grounds the exploration in rigorous scholarship but also invites readers to consider how these diverse voices contribute to a holistic understanding of the wounded feminine. By weaving together these definitions and inspirations, this book sets the stage for a comprehensive and illuminating journey into reclaiming and reimagining the Wounded Mother archetype in contemporary discourse.

Terms and Definitions

Internalized Negative Mother: An inner critical voice or negative energy that causes self-doubt and feelings of inadequacy. This can stem from personal experiences or the pervasive negative aspects of the mother archetype.

Mother Archetype: A fundamental concept representing the maternal figure, encompassing both positive and negative aspects. This archetype exhibits inherent ambivalence. Negative aspects include associations with the secret, hidden, dark, the abyss, the world of the dead, anything that devours, seduces, poisons, is terrifying, and inescapable.

Mother-Complex: A psychological complex formed from the mother archetype, manifesting in both sons and daughters with varied effects. A negative mother-complex in daughters can result in resistance to the mother and difficulties in building her own life.

"Mom" Stereotype: A contemporary societal caricature of an unhappy, anxious, and victimized mother figure, reflecting a potentially wounded aspect of the archetype in the collective consciousness.

Primal Relationship and Fear: The infant's early dependence on the mother, an archetypal relationship. Negative experiences within this relationship can lead to the child perceiving the mother as the "terrible" mother, lacking security, and fostering a sense of wounding.

Projection: The attribution of traits and impacts to the personal mother that originate from the archetype rather than her actual character. A "wounded" mother figure in an individual's psyche may reflect a projection of the negative aspects of the mother archetype.

Shadow of Motherhood: The repressed "dark," unruly, and frightening aspects of the maternal experience due to cultural idealization of motherhood. Acknowledging and integrating this shadow is crucial for understanding the full spectrum of the mother archetype, including its wounded expressions.
Terrible Mother (Archetype): An archetype embodying the possessive, imprisoning, depriving, and devouring aspects of the feminine. Fear of the feminine is often linked to this manifestation.

Traumatic Conditions: Effects similar to those of personal trauma, produced by the significant determining power of archetypal motifs. A lack of connection to the archetypal motive forces within mythological and religious spheres can be a cause of disturbance.

Two-Faced Maternity: The ambivalent nature of the mother image, appearing both playful/generous and treacherous/sinister. This duality is inherent to the archetype itself.

Unmothered Experience: A personal history of having a physically or emotionally unavailable mother, leading to unresolved issues and feelings of abandonment and isolation, particularly when the individual becomes a parent. Contributes to the experience of a wounded maternal archetype internally.

"Witch/Bruja (Brew-Ha)" as Archetype: During a child's development toward independence, the mother figure in the primal relationship may be experienced as a "witch/Bruja" – a restrictive power to be overcome. This reflects an archetypal dynamic, not necessarily the personal mother's character. A "witch/Bruja" (Brew-Ha) represents a multifaceted figure or concept. While often depicted as an evil symbol associated with danger, magic, spirits, and the Terrible Mother archetype, it also embodies aspects of the dark feminine, the shadow side of the personality, and powerful instinctual knowledge. Figures like Baba Yaga and the witches as spinners/weavers suggest a connection to creation, transformation, and wisdom, sometimes helpful, sometimes terrifying, reflecting the complex and ambivalent nature of these archetypal energies.

PART I: UNDERSTANDING THE WOUNDED MOTHER ARCHETYPE

In order to fully reclaim and heal the Wounded Feminine, it is essential to first understand the roots of the Wounded Mother archetype and how it operates within both the personal and collective psyche. This section provides a foundational exploration of the feminine wound, the Great Mother archetype, and the ways in which the Wounded Mother functions as a "lifesystem" within individuals and communities. Through this analysis, readers are invited to consider how patriarchal systems, cultural erasure, and historical trauma have contributed to the neglect and fragmentation of the feminine, particularly for Women of Color. By tracing these wounds back to their source, this section lays the groundwork for transformative healing.

Chapter One

THE FEMININE WOUND

As a Wounded Mother, these are the experiences that resonate with me, that I see reflected in my own journey, and in the journeys of so many others: My body... It holds so much. The searing, unforgettable pain of childbirth, a kind of primal fire that changes you forever. Then, the monthly reminder of my vulnerability, the bleeding that feels, at times, like a shameful secret, a messy truth we're taught to hide. There's a deep resonance with the image of Our Lady of the Sick, "a God who bleeds."[1] She understands this body, this messy, painful, miraculous vessel. She helps me try to heal this fractured relationship with my own flesh and blood. Motherhood has been my crucible. It has tested me, broken me open, and reshaped me in ways I never imagined. I've felt lost in the chaos, drowning in despair, disconnected from myself, and even, in my darkest moments, from my own children. The weight of it all... the feeling of being trapped, utterly depleted. Postpartum depression isn't just a clinical term; it's a living nightmare, a suffocating darkness where I lost myself. And even without that diagnosis, there's this constant erosion, this slow, insidious process of "losing ourselves" in the face of demands that never cease. Those old wounds, the ones I carried from childhood, they've been ripped open again, exposed in new and terrifying ways as I try to navigate this uncharted territory of being a parent.

The wounding goes deeper than just the physical and the mental. It's a severing, a cutting away of something essential. My feminine instincts, that natural wisdom that should guide me, feel muffled, silenced. I feel like I've "lost my voice," that I can't speak my truth, that my own needs and desires are irrelevant. The image of the "handless maiden" chills me to the bone. It speaks to that feeling of powerlessness, of having my ability to act, to shape my own world, stolen from me. That wounding, often inflicted by the "father"—whether a literal

1 *See Tim Staples, Behold Your Mother (Catholic Answers Press, 2017).*

figure or the crushing weight of patriarchal culture—leaves me feeling like a ghost of myself. The scars of my past haunt my present. The adverse childhood experiences, the parental abuse... they cast a long shadow over my motherhood. I've walked through a "dark passage," reliving those feelings of abandonment, of being utterly alone. Healing from that kind of trauma is like trying to break free from a curse, a long, agonizing process of reclaiming my shattered self, and even the mother-child relationship, the bond that's supposed to be the most sacred, can be a source of pain, of deep disturbance. When a child's own instincts are twisted, it creates a kind of psychic battleground, where terrifying fantasies take root and poison the connection between us. The world I live in... it devalues everything I am. The feminine, in all its forms, is seen as less than, as weak, as other. This historical and cultural devaluation seeps into my bones, making me doubt my own worth, my own femininity. I'm afraid to embrace my "authentic Self," to be who I truly am, because I know it will be met with judgment, with scorn. The patriarchal ideals, the suffocating expectations, they threaten to crush the wildness within me, that Lilith-like part of myself that refuses to be tamed. And even within myself, I struggle against the mother archetype, rejecting those obscure, instinctive, unconscious parts of my own nature, the very parts that hold the key to my power. The myth of Eve, the blame placed on women for the "Fall," it's a constant reminder of this historical wound, this fallen condition that's been imposed on us for centuries.

The Mother Wound [2] refers to the deep, often unspoken emotional and psychological pain or trauma that arises from a mother's inability—whether through her own wounds, systemic oppression, cultural conditioning, or absence—to provide the consistent emotional nurturing and attunement a child needs. It's not about blaming individual mothers but

2 See Bethany Webster, *Discovering the Inner Mother* (HarperCollins, 2021).

about acknowledging and healing the generational patterns that are passed down, especially through the feminine line.

Core Aspects of the Mother Wound

Emotional Abandonment or Neglect: Not feeling seen, heard, or emotionally supported.

Conditional Love: Feeling loved only when meeting certain expectations or roles.

Silencing or Shame: Being discouraged from expressing anger, grief, or authentic feelings.

Insecurity or People-Pleasing: Learning to earn love through performance or self-erasure.

Lack of Modeling for Self-Love: Growing up without examples of healthy boundaries, emotional regulation, or self-worth.

Spiritual and Cultural Layers: For many Women of Color, Queer individuals, or those from marginalized communities, the Mother Wound is entangled with systemic forces—colonialism, patriarchy, racism, poverty, and intergenerational trauma. These layers can distort mothering itself, where survival takes precedence over nurture.

I've come to understand the Mother Wound not simply as a personal ache, but as a collective rupture that lives in the bones and breath of women like me—Women of Color, queer women, mothers shaped by survival and silence. Within my own soul, I have carried the weight of this wound, not always knowing its name, but always feeling its impact—in the exhaustion that feels ancestral, in the silence I inherited, and in the deep yearning to be both held and whole. For us, the pain of the Mother Wound doesn't emerge in isolation. It is braided into larger systems—colonialism, patriarchy, racism, poverty—that have for generations dictated how we mother, how we love, how we survive. I grew up in a world where survival often came first, and nurturing—soft, sacred nurturing—was a privilege, not a given. Many of our mothers and grandmothers did what they could with what they had. They loved us fiercely, but sometimes that love came wrapped in discipline, distance, or duty. The soft was often sacrificed for the strong. Lisa Marchiano writes about the internalized "negative mother,"[3] a voice that whispers we are never enough, especially when we are stretched thin, unseen, and trying to pour from an empty vessel. I've heard that voice—while rocking a crying baby, while trying to love through my own trauma, while staring into the mirror wondering if I could really offer something different. That voice was not just my own. It echoed generations. And when I became a mother, that echo grew louder. The child in me remembered what it meant to feel alone. Motherhood, for many of us, is a reckoning. It surfaces every hidden shadow: abandonment, shame, resentment, the fear of repeating what we swore we'd escape. And all of that is amplified when layered with systemic oppression. As a Latina woman raised in the Bronx, I know what it feels like to live in the margins. Our communities have always been shaped by more than love—they've been shaped by labor, exploitation, sterilization, surveillance. The state often parented us before our own parents could.

The pain of being unseen is doubled when society already sees you as a problem, a burden, a stereotype. As Christena Cleveland writes, we were born into a world designed by the "white male god"—a cold, anti-nurturing system that teaches

3 *See Lisa Marchiano, MOTHERHOOD: Facing and Finding Yourself (CO: Sounds True, 2021).*

us that to need is to be weak, and to be Black, brown, or woman is to be expendable. For Black women especially, the "Strong Black Woman" archetype may be armor, but it is also a cage. It silences vulnerability in the name of survival. It is praised publicly and punished privately. This is what we inherit, and yet, this is also where we begin to heal. Because even in these harsh conditions, we have found ways to love. Mujerista theology reminds us that survival itself is a sacred act. In our barrios, in our kitchens, in our whispers and songs, we create new ways of caring. We mother one another. We make altars out of broken things. We turn trauma into testimony. The Mother Wound is not just what was lost—it is also what we are reclaiming. We are re-parenting ourselves. We are listening to our inner children. We are choosing to nurture even when we were never nurtured. We are making space for grief and calling it holy. Yes, the systems are real. The struggle is daily. But so is the strength. So is the softness returning to our spirits. So is the love that rises when we finally see ourselves not as broken, but as becoming.

Healing the Mother Wound: Re-parenting the Inner Child: Learning to nurture and protect the parts of yourself that were unseen or harmed.

Grieving What Was Missing: Honoring the loss without guilt or shame.

Breaking the Cycle: Choosing new ways of being with yourself, your children, and your community.

Spiritual Reclamation: Reconnecting with a Divine Feminine, Earth Mother, or spiritual source of unconditional love.

Healing my Mother Wound—especially as it intersects with the larger systems of marginalization I've lived through—has never been a neat or linear process. It's not about curing something broken. It's a messy, sacred, and ongoing process of internal transformation, reckoning with my past, confronting hard truths, and opening to relationships and community in ways I didn't think were possible. I had to confront the wound. Facing the pain head-on meant revisiting experiences I tried to bury—moments of abandonment, shame, silence. I had to look at my own darkness and stop pretending I wasn't hurting. There was no bypassing it. The only way out was through. I realized that healing demanded I live through the complexity of the wound—feel it, name it, and lean into it. I started to make meaning out of my disappointments and fractured narratives. That was the beginning of reclaiming myself.

Motherhood—literal or metaphorical—became a crucible.
It challenged every outdated part of me. Parts of my personality that were born to survive no longer fit. I descended into deep places within my psyche, meeting my shadow, and sometimes, it was terrifying. But it was also fertile. In those dark places, I started to uncover the possibility of becoming more whole. Letting go of my former self—those layers of performance and protection—allowed me to be reborn in some ways, into a fuller, more grounded version of who I am.

I learned to gather up the fragmented parts of me—the angry parts, the tired parts, the needy parts I had tried to suppress. I began to see them not as flaws, but as wisdom-bearing aspects of my psyche. Like alchemy, the inner work turned rage into resilience, grief into grounding. The spiritual journey became one of gathering the lost pieces and stitching together a soul that could hold complexity. And I began to accept my need. I'd been conditioned to see need as weakness—especially as a woman of color living under systems that pathologize vulnerability. But I learned that reclaiming my need was a radical act. I gave myself permission to say what I felt, to ask for what I needed, to be held. The pain of loneliness, when acknowledged, softened. I didn't need to be unbreakable to be worthy. My very humanness became sacred ground.

Relationship and community held me through it. Healing wasn't something I could do alone. I found—sometimes stumbled into—people who were also carrying their wounds. And together, in spaces of honesty and courage, we began to build something healing. Not perfect, but real. We made room for our pain, our softness, our becoming. These were not spaces of pity, but of power. We didn't try to erase the pain; we let it shape us into better listeners, better kin. We learned that repair mattered as much as connection—when things broke, we found ways to come back. The spiritual dimensions of this healing came alive too. I encountered energies and archetypes that whispered truths into my journey—the Sacred Black Feminine, Sophia, Our Lady of the Sick. They welcomed my need, affirmed my dignity, and reminded me that wisdom lives in the wound. I began to understand myself as a "wounded healer"—not despite my pain, but because of it. The more I honored the pain in my own heart, the more capacity I had to hold space for others. And that, too, was healing.

I had to redefine what care means. In communities like mine, where survival is often the main priority, nurture doesn't always look like softness. It can look like showing up, feeding each other, holding sacred rage, building sanctuary in the middle of systems that want us erased. We mothered through protest, through song, through laughter, through showing up again and again. Our care practices weren't always gentle—but they were rooted in deep love. So yes, healing the Mother Wound has meant turning toward pain rather than running from it. It's meant piecing together a life with the tools I have—curiosity, empathy, playfulness, honesty. It's about daring to see myself whole. And perhaps most sacredly, it's been about learning that the places I once felt most broken are the same places where I now feel most connected—to myself, to others, and to something much deeper than words. These wounds, this multifaceted pain—physical, psychological, relational, cultural—are brought into sharp focus by motherhood. It's a catalyst, a crucible that forces us to confront the deepest, most hidden parts of ourselves. Yet, even in this darkness, there's a glimmer of hope. This journey through the wounded landscape of motherhood can also be a path to transformation, to healing, to reclaiming my authority, my instincts. Facing the "dark feminine," embracing the challenges, can lead to a profound connection with my own inner wisdom, a reorientation of my values. I'm learning that I must face my shadow, those disowned, unacceptable parts of myself, in order to grow. And in this process, I'm finding connection—to my child, to other mothers, to the women who came before me, a lineage of strength and resilience. I'm beginning to understand the concept of the "wounded healer," that my pain, as human as it is, can lead to a deeper self-realization, a more profound understanding of myself and my place in the world.

Chapter Two

THE GREAT MOTHER ARCHETYPE

I've come to recognize the Great Mother Archetype as a deep, universal pattern that lives within me and within us all—regardless of gender, orientation, or identity. It is a powerful, inborn image rooted in our shared psychological heritage. For me, it isn't just a symbol of maternity or womanhood—it is an energetic principle, a matrix of life itself, that undergirds both the personal and the collective journey of becoming. Alongside the archetype of the hero, the Great Mother represents one of the foundational paths of human psychic experience. Her presence gives rise to what Jungian psychology calls the "mother-complex," [1] and I've come to see how this plays out in subtle and obvious ways within my own story and the stories of others I hold space for—especially those of us who identify within the LGBTQI+ spectrum.

Nature and Origin

The Great Mother is not just a personal figure—it is an eternal form that shapes our psychic structure. She emerges from a wellspring of instinctual wisdom so ancient that encountering her evokes awe, reverence, and sometimes fear. While the religious imagination may describe her as a goddess or as the Divine Feminine, I feel her more as an atmosphere—a presence that contains all life and death, nurture and danger, visibility and concealment. For me, she often appears not as my personal mother but as a force moving through the people, dreams, and symbols of my life. Even when I see her in a physical mother, a lover, a drag queen, or the land beneath my feet, I know I am touching something older than any of us—something sacred. She can show up in queer elders, femme ancestors, or genderqueer mentors whose care shaped my becoming. In those moments, the mythic weight she carries becomes clear.

---

1 See Carl G. Jung, *The Archetypes and the Collective Unconscious* (NJ: Princeton University Press, 1959).

Manifestations and Symbols

This archetype takes on an almost infinite variety of forms—some familiar, some strange. She appears in personal figures: mothers, grandmothers, stepmothers, and caretakers. But she also arrives through goddesses like Kali, Isis, Sophia, and the Black Madonna; through places like the sea, forests, cities, and sacred wells; and through symbols like the moon, the rose, the womb, and the vessel. For LGBTQI+ folks, she sometimes appears through chosen family—the queer mother who protected us when our own mothers couldn't, the ballroom mother who taught us to walk in our truth, the elder who midwifed us through gender transition, or the nonbinary Earth who holds us when we feel unheld. She is present in every kitchen table where we're fed without judgment, every healing circle, every glitter-stained ritual space where our full selves are welcomed. She is the shelter we create for one another. She is also symbolized in the sacred and hollow spaces—wells, vessels, and deep places within the psyche where transformation happens. She is the dark cave, the drag closet, the quiet breath before coming out. Even the body, in all its fluidity, becomes a temple of her mystery.

Her Ambivalence: The Loving and The Terrible Mother

I've encountered both her tenderness and her terror. The Great Mother holds the paradox of creation and destruction. Her loving side is the source of nourishment, protection, and radical welcome. She is the maternal instinct that transcends gender. She is the one who fosters our growth, whispers sacred wisdom in dreams, and sustains us through grief. I've seen her in the kindness of a nurse, the touch of a lover, the sacred ritual of gender-affirming care, and the quiet dignity of surviving in a world not made for us. But she also comes with shadow. She can be suffocating, possessive, and terrifying. In moments of abandonment, shame, or religious trauma, I've felt her as a devouring force—a witch, a void, a paralyzing fear. For many LGBTQI+ people, especially those of us rejected by our families or faith traditions, she shows up as the terrible mother—the one who shuns, controls, or punishes. She is the archetype behind the internalized voice that says we are too much, not enough, unworthy. The inner work is learning to recognize her shadow, to name it, and to reclaim our power from it. Yet even her darkness is a gate. She invites us to descend into the underworld of the soul, to face death and rebirth, and to rise transformed. In her terrible form, she is the initiator—teaching us boundaries, sovereignty, and the sacred art of letting go.

Psychological Significance and Function

The Great Mother lives at the root of our psychic development. As children, we begin life in her domain—completely held, surrounded by the feminine. This early bond can be nurturing or wounding, and it shapes how we relate to others and to ourselves. Many of us, especially queer and trans folks, must navigate complex mother-complexes: longing for nurture while fearing control, idealizing the feminine while feeling betrayed by it, desiring connection yet needing separation. As I've walked this path, I've learned that healing the mother wound is not about returning to the literal mother—it's about reclaiming the inner archetypal Mother in a way that is life-giving. For queer people, this often involves creating new rituals, new language, new spiritual paths that allow us to experience the Great Mother in forms that affirm who we are. She may come as a queer priestess, a fluid Earth deity, a trans goddess, or as the Spirit of Wisdom beyond binaries.

A Wounded Mother

The Great Mother is the matrix from which consciousness is born. The hero in me must eventually face her, not to destroy her, but to wrest from her the jewel of selfhood. Every time I return from the dark depths with new insight, I carry her essence with me—fertile, transformative, and whole. For those of us who live outside the lines—whether by identity, calling, or choice—the Great Mother is both a home and a horizon. She is the sacred well of origin and the dark womb of becoming. When I honor her, I honor the Divine within myself—the part of me that creates, nurtures, dreams, and destroys in order to give birth to something more real.

Chapter Three

THE WOUNDED MOTHER AS A LIFESYSTEM

A Wounded Mother

Rather than viewing the Wounded Mother solely as an individual experience, this chapter presents her as a "lifesystem" [1]—a dynamic and interconnected force that influences emotional, psychological, and communal well-being. Just as ecosystems suffer when key elements are disrupted, the Wounded Mother archetype reflects a broader imbalance that affects relationships, self-worth, and societal structures. Healing the Wounded Mother requires a paradigm shift—one that moves beyond simple notions of personal trauma toward an understanding of cycles, renewal, and interconnectedness. This chapter introduces metaphors of life cycles, the seasons, and regenerative healing, illustrating how the process of restoring the Wounded Mother mirrors natural rhythms. Just as forests regenerate after fires and rivers carve new paths through landscapes, the inner work of reclaiming the Wounded Feminine is both a destruction of the old and a birth of the new. Through this framework, readers are encouraged to see healing not as a linear process but as a cyclical one, requiring continuous engagement with shadow work, self-nurturing, and communal support. By embracing the Wounded Mother as a system in need of restoration rather than as a static or broken archetype, this chapter lays the foundation for a transformative journey—one that moves toward wholeness, balance, and a reimagined relationship with the feminine.

Once, there was a Mother who held the whole world in her body. She wasn't the kind of mother you'd find in stained glass or seated on a throne of halos. She was the earth beneath your feet—the soil, the blood, the wind, the weeping. She was the whisper of roots beneath the surface, the stillness before a storm, the warmth in a kitchen at midnight. Her body gave life not only in birth, but in every act of holding, feeding,

1 See Melanie L Harris, Ecowomanism : African American Women and Earth-Honoring Faiths (Maryknoll (Ny): Orbis Books, 2017).

forgiving, and letting go. But one day, the world she nurtured slipped through her fingers. It wasn't a single moment, but a slow unraveling of forgetting. Her children, once nourished by her care, began building walls instead of gardens. They mistook her pain for weakness, her silence for absence, her tenderness for liability. And when she cried, they cursed the weather. When she shook, they called it disaster. She had given everything—milk, breath, shelter, song—and still, they turned away. So she began to break. Not out of bitterness, but from the unbearable ache of being unseen. The rivers within her dried like closing veins. The forests grew silent. The birds forgot their flight paths. Deep within her belly, something ancient curled in mourning—the part of her that once believed that love alone could hold everything together.

I know this story because I, too, have lived it. I have carried life only to feel it slip from me. I have poured from a cup that never refilled. I have been that Mother, whose wounds bled invisibly while the world expected more. And I have learned—slowly, painfully, beautifully—that when a Mother begins to grieve, the whole system feels it. Because she is not separate from the system. She is the system. Her body is not just metaphor, but the actual ecology of healing and harm, connection and collapse. Every relationship she touches, every silence she swallows, forms the weather of the heart and the climate of the spirit. But this is not the end of the story. Even in her brokenness, the Mother is not forsaken. Her grief becomes compost—rich, fertile, holy. Her tears nourish the buried parts of herself, and new life rises from what was once thought to be ruin. Flowers bloom from fault lines. Trees root themselves in scar tissue. And slowly, she remembers: her value was never in her productivity, but in her presence. Her sacredness is not diminished by her pain. It is made visible through it.

A Wounded Mother

Theopoetically, She is a Wounded Mother. She is a Lifesystem, and when she chooses herself—her rest, her voice, her softness—the world begins to breathe again. Children/innerchild who had forgotten how to listen begin to hear. The ones who left return—not to take, but to tend. Healing becomes a shared harvest. The land within and the land without pulse in rhythm once more. This is the sacred ecology of healing: the divine truth that nurturing the world begins with learning to mother oneself. So, if you, beloved, find yourself breaking—do not despair. The Wounded Mother in you is not the end. She is the threshold. The beginning. The soil from which a new world can finally grow.

PART II: THE INNER FEMININE & THE WOUND

The wounds of the Wounded Mother archetype are not merely external; they are deeply embedded within the psyche, shaping how individuals relate to themselves, their emotions, and their sense of worth. Part II shifts the focus inward, exploring how the feminine within has been neglected, silenced, and diminished, particularly for Women of Color navigating complex layers of oppression and expectation. This section acknowledges the pain of internalized wounds while also offering pathways for nurturing and liberation. Through Theopoetic storytelling, psychological insights, and spiritual practices, readers will be guided toward a compassionate reconnection with their inner feminine, learning to embrace self-love as an act of personal and collective transformation.

Chapter Four

THE NEGLECTED FEMININE WITHIN

I've come to know the Neglected Feminine Within not just as a theory or a cultural critique, but as a very real absence I've felt in my bones and in my soul. She is the part of me—and the part of the world—that has been ignored, suppressed, misunderstood, or outright denied. For a long time, I didn't have language for what I was sensing: a longing, a gap, an ache for something sacred that had been buried beneath layers of patriarchy, theology, and fear. But as I've journeyed inward, and listened to the whispers of dreams, ancestors, and my own body, I've begun to recognize her—the forgotten feminine, both human and divine. She once had names. Sophia. Lilith. Anima. The Black Madonna.[1] She once had temples and songs and myths. But somewhere along the way, those names were erased or twisted, and her presence became shadow. In the spiritual traditions I inherited, Sophia[2]—the Divine Wisdom—was veiled, made silent, and cast into theological footnotes. They called her the Holy Spirit, but never mother. They spoke of her as inspiration, but never incarnation. She remained in the tradition, yes, but she was blackened, ignored, and hidden away. It was as if the Western world had been orphaned of the Goddess—and we've been reeling from that loss ever since.

Sophia still comes to me, though—especially in dreams. But she doesn't always come gently. She comes veiled in grief, cloaked in mystery, draped in shadow. She is the Dark Mother and the Lady of the Perfect Black—the one who has suffered everything humanity has suffered, and who still sings, not despite the pain, but through it. Her wisdom isn't logical or linear. It's instinctive, bodily, intuitive. And maybe that's why she has been feared for so long—because you can't control her. You can only surrender to her rhythm. I've also

---

1 *See Christena Cleveland, God Is a Black Woman (New York: Harperone, 2022).*

2 *See Caitlin Matthews, Sophia: Goddess of Wisdom, Bride of God (Quest Books, 2013).*

met Lilith [3] —not the demon they warned me about, but the untamed, exiled part of me that never bowed to what didn't feel true. Lilith is that raw, instinctual side of the feminine that patriarchal culture tried to shame out of me. She's not polite. She doesn't play small. She carries rage, yes—but it's a holy rage. Her refusal to be subjugated wasn't sin. It was survival. And in her, I recognize the parts of myself that were called "too much," "too loud," "too sexual," "too wild." But what if those parts were never wrong? What if they were sacred all along?

For those of us raised in deeply gendered, hierarchical systems, the inner feminine was often cast as weakness or temptation. As a man, I was taught to project my anima onto women, to worship or fear them in extremes—to see them either as angel or seductress, saint or swamp witch. And because I wasn't taught to tend to the inner Sophia in me, I kept her locked away in my unconscious. But what I've learned is this: when we don't consciously relate to the feminine within us, we live in exile from our own souls. We chase projections instead of presence. We mistake dominance for strength. We confuse control with love. And for the women I know and walk with, the story is just as tragic. Raised in a culture that devalues the feminine, many have felt estranged from their own inner depths. They've had to survive by over-identifying with masculine ideals of success, power, and logic—often at the cost of intuition, sensuality, receptivity, and the knowing of the body. In trying to become what the world told them they needed to be, they've sometimes lost sight of who they truly are. They weren't just cut off from their mothers; they were cut off from the Mother of All.

This disconnection isn't just personal—it's cultural and systemic. The Divine Feminine was submerged beneath centuries of

---

3 *See Barbara Black Koltuv, The Book of Lilith (FL: Nicolas-Hays, Inc., 1986).*

patriarchal theology and philosophy. She was reframed as problem, temptation, error. The very structure of Western consciousness—its obsession with conquest, clarity, and linear progress—reflects a masculine orientation that has overshadowed the cyclical, the intuitive, the relational. The result is imbalance, both within individuals and the world. But here's the truth I've come to hold sacred: She's not gone. She's waiting. The Neglected Feminine Within is not dead—she's dreaming. And now, she is stirring. In dreams. In rituals. In revolutions. In the voices of the outcast. In the breath of queer bodies reclaiming sacred space. In the aching of the Earth. In our collective longing for wholeness.

She is the source of the hidden mysteries that are now rising to the surface—not to return us to the past, but to rebalance what has been broken. To restore the lost song. To remind us that the holy is not only above but within—within our bodies, our feelings, our wounds, our desires, our sacred, shattered feminine hearts. And so, I listen. I let her speak again. Through story. Through silence. Through shadow. Through me.

A Theopoetic Expression:

There once lived a quiet Presence deep within my soul—soft, fluid, and ancient as moonlight on still water. She was the Feminine Within: the keeper of intuition, dream, feeling, and the sacred rhythm of becoming. She didn't speak in declarations, but in the hush between my heartbeats, in the warm weight of tears I had not yet cried, in the deep urge to rest even when the world demanded more of me. Over time, I began to silence her. Not out of cruelty, but out of survival. Her voice was called irrational. Her knowing dismissed. Her cycles were seen as inconvenient. Her softness mistaken for weakness. Her sensuality was something to fear, even within myself. Slowly, she faded, like a song I once loved but no longer played. She became a ghost in the house of my own being. The masculine within me—structured, praised, and rewarded—took over. I built systems to manage my pain, wore productivity like armor, and learned how to live in constant motion. I thought strength meant ignoring the ache, the fatigue, the longing. And all the while, the Feminine Within waited. She waited in my dreams. She waited in the anxiety that lived in my chest. She waited in my sudden weeping at poetry, in the ache that no accomplishment could soothe. Her silence was never absence—it was an invitation.

Then one day, I blossomed like a flower. Not from violence, but from surrender. Maybe it was the heartbreak I couldn't name, the exhaustion I could no longer numb, or the sacred silence of a long walk beneath the stars. Whatever it was, something inside me gave way. From that fracture, she rose—not angry, but aching. Not vengeful, but weary of being cast aside. She didn't scold me. She didn't shout. She simply whispered, "Sit with me. Feel this. Rest. Remember." And so, I began to listen. I learned to honor my inner rhythm, not just my responsibilities. Dreams became sacred maps. Emotions became waters I learned to float in, not drown beneath. I no longer feared the dark—because she taught me it was also fertile. The Feminine Within didn't return to destroy the life I had built—she returned to nourish it. She braided together the pieces of me I had left behind: the mystic, the mother, the artist, the lover. She reminded me that healing is not linear, and wholeness is not perfection—it is integration. Now, I tend the altar within my soul where she dwells. I offer her time, tenderness, creativity, and space. I walk with both softness and strength, with intuition and clarity. The neglected Feminine is no longer silent in me—she is sacred. She is seen. And with her, I am learning to be whole again.

Chapter Five

NURTURING THE UNNATURED

A Wounded Mother

I've come to understand the deep and often hidden work of nurturing the unnurtured—even if I didn't always call it that. For me, this journey means tending to the wounded, silenced, or forgotten parts of myself, others, and even the divine. It's a path of healing and reintegration—of listening to what's been ignored, reclaiming what's been cast off, and allowing love to return to what has been left unloved. At times, I've felt unmoored from my own instincts, struggling to navigate life—especially in roles like mothering or mentoring—because I was disconnected from the quiet inner voices that once guided me. I've learned that nurturing begins with trusting those inner promptings, those irrational yearnings that so many systems have taught me to silence. I now honor the regenerative power of the unconscious, letting it work in dreams, in stillness, in the spaces where I no longer try to control everything.

Motherhood—whether literal or symbolic—has resurfaced old pain from when I felt "unmothered," emotionally abandoned, or unseen. But these moments became gateways. The resurfacing of that pain invited me to sit with my wounded inner child, to tend to her, and to finally offer the care she never received. It wasn't easy, but in that mess, I found the possibility of renewal. I've also come to know the archetype of the Wounded Healer[1] —the idea that the very places I've been broken can become sources of healing for others. In claiming my own wounds, not denying them or covering them in shame, I found a kind of sacred responsibility: to walk beside others in their pain, not because I have all the answers, but because I've been there too.

Part of my healing required me to look into the shadow—the parts of myself I'd cast out or judged too ugly, too much, too irrational. In fairy tales, healing often happens in the dirty water, the ugly flower, the blackened space—and I've

1 See Henri J M Nouwen, *The Wounded Healer* (New York Doubleday , 1979).

learned that those images aren't just stories. They are symbols of the transformation that happens when we stop running and begin to tend the hidden places within us. This isn't just personal work—it's collective. I see it in liberation movements, in Paulo Freire's insistence that the oppressed must reclaim their humanity by becoming beings for themselves, not objects for others. His pedagogy of the oppressed [2] echoes what I've come to know: that love, critical consciousness, and creative action are forms of nurturing that restore dignity and wholeness to individuals and communities flattened by systems of domination. True teaching doesn't fill us up like empty vessels—it awakens us.

I see this too in the voices of women like Gloria Anzaldúa, who speak of being "culturally crucified," [3] yet still carry the fierce instinct to nurture others from a place of deep, ancestral knowing. In her, in Lupe, in all the women who mother the world even when the world has denied them, I see the Divine Feminine rising—not as a distant ideal, but as an instinctual, embodied wisdom. Nurturing the unnurtured, then, is a radical act. It's a reclamation of what's been lost in me and around me. It means learning to love what has been cast out, to trust what has been called irrational, and to offer presence where there has been absence. It's a lifelong process of healing, integrating, and liberating—of becoming whole in a world that has often tried to fracture me.

---

2 *See Paulo Freire, Pedagogy of the Oppressed (NY: Continuum International Publishing Group, 2011).*

3 *See Gloria Anzaldúa, Borderlands / La Frontera : The New Mestiza (San Francisco: Aunt Lute Books, 1999).*

Chapter Six

LOVE AS LIBERATION

The concept of Love as Liberation lives in me—not as something abstract or sentimental, but as something deeply embodied, fiercely committed, and intimately tied to my own journey of becoming free. It's not just an emotion I feel. It's a force that moves me, sustains me, and calls me into action—personally, collectively, and spiritually.

Love as the Root and Fire of My Freedom

I've come to realize that love is the condition that makes liberation possible. Love creates the ground for dialogue, and dialogue opens the path to humanization. Without love, there can be no freedom. For me, love isn't soft or sweet all the time—it's an act of courage. It's a choice I make every day to remain open, present, and willing to struggle for the dignity of others and myself. In my solidarity with those who suffer, I've entered into painful truths, not because it's easy, but because love makes it necessary. To stand in someone else's shoes, to risk comfort and control in service of transformation—that's love. That's liberation. I've learned that even my response to violence or oppression can be rooted in love when it arises from a desire to reclaim my humanity. I don't want to be a victim of dehumanization, and I don't want to pass it on to others. Love helps me break that cycle. For me, liberation isn't some separate spiritual salvation—it's woven into how I love my neighbor, how I show up in community, and how I relate to the Divine. Especially as a woman of color, salvation and liberation are inseparable.

The Divine Love That Sets Me Free

When I invoke the Divine, I don't imagine a distant, punitive figure. I connect with Sophia [1] —the Black Woman God, [2] the Divine Feminine who moves through the world in waves of burning, protective, intelligent love. She doesn't shame or control me. She guides me, shelters me, empowers me. Her love doesn't seek obedience; it seeks my freedom. To know that I am seen, sought after, and cherished by this kind of love—especially when I'm stuck in the "mud" of life—is the beginning of my liberation. I can surrender to Her love without fear. I can trust that I am inherently worthy, even when white patriarchal systems tell me otherwise. That's a revolution. That's healing. Being alive, for me, is proof that I am loved. And it's only because I have been set free by this love that I can extend freedom to others.

Becoming Free to Love Authentically

Liberation, for me, isn't just about breaking chains—it's about rewiring how I relate. I've had to unlearn patterns of hiding, shrinking, and performing. Freedom means I can bring my full self into relationships. It means I can offer love without losing myself. As I grow in awareness—what Freire called conscientization—I take responsibility for my freedom. I'm not just reacting anymore. I'm choosing, acting, reflecting. This awareness creates space within me, and from that space, I can offer hospitality to others—not just in physical ways, but in the soulful sense of making room for their presence, their truth. In doing this, I move beyond love that is distorted by patriarchy—love that asks me to endure abuse or erase myself for the sake of others. I want the kind of love that liberates, not the kind that binds.

---

1 *See Caitlin Matthews, Sophia: Goddess of Wisdom, Bride of God (Quest Books, 2013).*

2 *See Christena Cleveland, God Is a Black Woman (New York: Harperone, 2022).*

Love and the Struggle for Wholeness

I've come to understand that love, like Eros, is paradoxical. It includes darkness and light. It wounds and heals. It's not always safe, but it always carries the possibility of rebirth. As Jung said, liberation is only possible from what we've possessed, done, or experienced. And I've experienced love's complexity—its ache and its grace. Through my own woundedness, I've found healing. I've turned pain into a source of nurture for others. That's what it means to be a wounded healer. I've been unnurtured, and now I can nurture. I can love in ways I wasn't loved, and that's part of my freedom. I also know how lonely the path can be when you resist injustice. But I've learned that even in that loneliness, love finds me—in community, in resistance, in tenderness. Solidarity is a kind of love that refuses to look away. For me, justice isn't dry policy—it's the flourishing of every human soul. It's joy. It's connection. It's being able to love and be loved fully and freely. Love is the journey, the struggle, and the destination. It drives me toward liberation, and it's what I discover when I get there. It asks everything of me—and gives everything in return. I am learning to live in that space, where love and freedom are one and the same.

PART III: THE WOUNDED MOTHER AS HEALER

Healing is not a linear process, nor is it solely an individual endeavor. The Wounded Mother archetype, once reclaimed, becomes a powerful source of transformation—not only for the self but also for others. Part III explores the profound shift that occurs when wounds are no longer seen as weaknesses but as doorways to deeper wisdom, resilience, and advocacy. By embracing vulnerability, standing in protection of the unprotected, and committing to an ongoing journey of integration, the Wounded Mother archetype emerges as both a healer and a guide. This section highlights the ways in which personal healing is intricately connected to collective liberation, inviting readers to see themselves as part of a greater web of transformation.

Chapter Seven

HEALING FROM VULNERBILITY

A Wounded Mother

For me, healing from vulnerability isn't about fixing what's broken or covering up what feels exposed. It's about learning to sit with the parts of myself that feel weak, wounded, and unsure—and realizing that those very parts can be sacred ground for transformation. Vulnerability isn't something I need to eliminate. Instead, I've come to understand it as a powerful doorway into deeper healing, connection, and ultimately, liberation. It starts with telling the truth about my woundedness. There have been moments when I've felt crippled at my core—cut off from others, from my own sense of self, and from hope. The shame of rejection or the ache of being misunderstood has sometimes left me feeling maimed. But I've learned that healing begins when I stop hiding those parts and instead walk them forward. I don't need to be "healed" to begin the journey. I just need to be honest about where I am.

Facing my pain has never been easy. It often means diving into uncomfortable, even repulsive places within—those dirty waters of fear, grief, or memory that I used to avoid. But when I lean in, when I choose to sit with that pain, something begins to shift. I start to reclaim pieces of myself I thought were lost. My fear becomes less a wall and more a teacher. In those moments, I discover what it means to be human and whole—messy, aching, but still breathing and reaching. What's surprised me most is that my wounds have become sources of strength. Like the archetype of the wounded healer, I've found that my suffering can offer wisdom—not just for me, but for others, too. When I share my pain, it loosens its grip. It becomes less of a weight and more of a bridge. Through that bridge, I can walk with others in their pain, not as someone who has all the answers, but as someone who knows the terrain. I've learned that being severed doesn't mean being beyond healing. It means I know how to be pieced back together—and I can help others do the same.

Relationships have been essential in this journey. Healing doesn't happen in isolation. I've needed the sacred presence of others—those who could hold space for my brokenness without trying to fix it. Hospitality, in its deepest form, has taught me that I don't have to pretend. I just need to show up, as I am, and trust that shared brokenness can become the ground of shared hope. And then there's the love—the kind that doesn't shame or control, but surrounds me like waves. Divine love, unconditional and relentless, has reminded me that being vulnerable doesn't make me weak. It makes me real. It invites me to embrace all of myself, even the parts I was taught to reject. That love helps me piece myself back together with tenderness, not judgment. And once I begin to feel that kind of love flow toward me, I find the strength to offer it to others. In the end, healing from vulnerability hasn't made me untouched by pain. It's made me open to transformation. My wounds have become openings—places where light and wisdom pour through. The cracks in my soul have become reminders of my strength. Liberation didn't come by pretending I wasn't broken. It came by loving myself enough to gather up the broken pieces and see them as holy.

Chapter Eight

PROTECTING THE UNPROTECTED

For me, protecting the unprotected isn't just an act of service—it's a calling that emerged from my own journey through pain, vulnerability, and healing. As I began to face and integrate my own wounds, something within me shifted. I couldn't just sit with my healing in isolation. The more I understood my own brokenness, the more I recognized the pain in others. I felt compelled—no, called—to step out and stand with those whose suffering mirrored my own, especially those society tends to ignore or silence. My healing taught me compassion—not a vague, distant kind, but the raw, aching compassion that comes from knowing what it means to be unseen or unsupported. I've carried loneliness. I've battled shame. I've felt the weight of rejection. And so, when I see others in those same shadows, my heart recognizes them as kin. I've learned to look into every face and see a neighbor. That's why I can't look away. I can't separate my healing from theirs. But I've also come to understand that this isn't something I can do alone. Protecting the unprotected is a shared task. It's not just about helping—it's about joining. It's about standing shoulder to shoulder with those who are struggling, not out of pity, but out of shared purpose. Liberation doesn't happen in isolation; it happens in solidarity. I've learned that if I want to be free, I have to work for the freedom of others too. This means being willing to take risks, to speak up, to act—not just for myself, but for a world where no one has to suffer in silence.

Creating spaces of safety and welcome has become sacred work for me. I've seen how healing happens when someone is simply allowed to be—when needs aren't hidden or shamed, but spoken and shared. Hospitality, in its deepest sense, is an act of resistance. In a world that punishes vulnerability, creating space for it becomes revolutionary. I try to build spaces—physical or spiritual—where people can come as they are, find their voice, and feel seen. Where loneliness can be named. Where pain can be held. Where community is formed from shared wounds, not in spite of them. But protecting the unprotected goes even further—it means confronting the systems that make people unprotected in the first place. This isn't about swooping in to save anyone. I've had to learn that real protection means walking with people as they claim their power. It means listening deeply, honoring their stories, and challenging the oppressive forces that silence them. I've had to unlearn the idea that I have the answers. Instead, I work to dismantle the structures that keep others from asking questions, from imagining new realities, from becoming the subjects of their own liberation. Sometimes it means speaking truth to power, even when it's uncomfortable—or dangerous. Sometimes it means staying in the room when I'd rather leave. Sometimes it means facing my own privilege or complicity. But every time I choose to protect the unprotected, I'm not just offering care—I'm reclaiming a part of my humanity. I'm remembering that healing is not just personal; it's political. It's spiritual. It's collective. To protect the unprotected is to say: You are not alone. Your needs are not a burden. Your pain is real. And your liberation matters as much as mine. It is to move from my own woundedness into a shared commitment to justice, to compassion, to transformation. This is the path I've chosen—and the one I keep walking.

Chapter Nine

A JOURNEY TOWARD WHOLENESS

A Wounded Mother

My journey toward wholeness—what many call the individuation process [1] —has been an ongoing unfolding, a lifelong invitation to integrate the fragments of who I am into something more complete, more true. I've come to understand that this is not about perfection, but about becoming who I've always been, beneath the masks and wounds. It's not linear or predictable; rather, it's a deeply irrational life-process, shaped by the language of symbols and the wisdom of the unconscious. For me, healing began with recognizing how much of my pain came from fragmentation—inner oppositions, disowned parts of myself, unresolved wounds. The work of healing, then, has been about integration: of light and shadow, masculine and feminine, conscious and unconscious. Each time I've touched the depths of my own suffering—my rage, loneliness, fear—I've also encountered the possibility of transformation. I've learned that wholeness doesn't come from erasing pain but from holding it with compassion, letting it become something generative rather than paralyzing. My wounds, when faced with awareness and care, have opened portals to new life.

To be human, I've discovered, is to be wounded—and it is through these very wounds that transformation takes place. Pain has taught me more than peace ever could. It has shown me how darkness is not just emptiness, but a fertile place where the seeds of new life germinate. I've had to meet my own shadow—those parts I once feared or despised—with a softness I never thought possible. In that encounter, something holy has always stirred. Rage has become fuel. Grief has become prayer. The ache in my chest has become a doorway to empathy. As I've walked this path, I've come to see how motherhood—literal or metaphorical—invites this sacred descent over and over. In the crucible of caring for

---

1 See C G Jung, Sonu Shamdasani, and Richard Francis, The Undiscovered Self with Symbols and the Interpretation of Dreams (NJ: Princeton University Press, 2011).

others, I've been confronted with my own limits, my projections, and my shadow. I've learned that to nurture another, I must first nurture myself. That the same fierce love I offer to others, I must offer to the child within me. That being present in the messiness, in the unsolvable tensions, is what allows me to grow. I've had to let go of the myth of the perfect mother or healer, and instead embrace the "terrible and loving mother" within—the one who holds both destruction and creation, terror and tenderness.

In moments of spiritual exhaustion, I've remembered that healing is cyclical. Just as day turns to night, I, too, must rest, reflect, and return. I've come to appreciate the stages: descent into the underworld of my soul, a sojourn in the unknown, and the slow, humble return with new wisdom. Sometimes that return takes years. Sometimes it comes with clarity; other times, with more questions. But I keep walking.

What grounds me now is a sense of purpose that emerges from my own suffering. In ministry, I don't come to "fix" others—I come as someone who has known pain, who still lives with it, and who has learned to let it speak. My heart breaks for those who suffer, and I know now that my own heartbreak is a sacred starting point. Through my wounds, I offer hospitality—not just the kind that welcomes someone into a space, but the kind that says, "I see your pain, and I am not afraid of it." This journey has required a fierce kind of tenderness. I've had to develop emotional literacy, to speak the language of my feelings with more honesty and nuance. I've had to sit with dreams and stories, rituals and memories, and let them reveal truths I couldn't reach any other way. I've had to feed the spiritual fire daily—gathering wood, tending the flame—because the sacred doesn't stay lit on its own.

A Wounded Mother

The Mother archetype, in all her mystery and multiplicity, has walked with me. Sometimes as a wise guide, sometimes as a shadowy figure, but always as a reminder that within me lives the capacity to hold grief and joy, terror and ecstasy. In her reflection, I've seen myself: wild, wounded, tender, strong. Self-healing isn't a final destination. It's a lifelong return to myself, again and again. And each time I return, I bring with me something more whole, more true, more alive.

PART IV: A WOMAN OF COLOR'S PERSPECTIVE ON THE ARCHETYPE

The journey of reclaiming the Wounded Mother archetype cannot be fully understood without examining the unique experiences of Women of Color. The wounds carried by these women are not only personal but deeply historical, cultural, and systemic. This section explores how generational trauma, colonial legacies, and intersectional oppression have shaped the feminine wound within communities of color. At the same time, it highlights the power of ancestral wisdom, decolonial perspectives, and sacred vulnerability as pathways toward healing. By centering the voices and experiences of Women of Color, this part of the book offers a nuanced understanding of the Wounded Mother archetype—one that is both deeply personal and universally resonant.

Chapter Ten

ANCESTRAL WOUNDS & FEMININE RECOVERY

For me, the journey toward wholeness as a woman of color means facing the deep ancestral wounds passed down through generations—wounds carved by histories of colonization, displacement, enslavement, and systemic oppression. These aren't just stories from the past—they live in my body, my choices, my silences, my fire. The pain is inherited, not by choice, but by bloodline, by spirit, by survival. I've learned that healing myself isn't just personal—it's collective. My pain echoes the pain of my foremothers who were gagged, sterilized, caged, and treated as expendable labor. I carry the memory of Chicana, Mexican, and Indigenous women whose bodies were colonized and whose voices were betrayed, not only by foreign powers but by their own communities. I hold in my soul the grief of Latinas who became strangers to themselves because they were taught that to survive, they had to forget who they were and be servants to a patriarchal system. I carry in my bones the exhaustion of being a Black woman expected to be unbreakable, shaped by stereotypes like Mammy, Jezebel, and Sapphire, while my real needs—my soft, human needs—were ignored or punished. I know the ache of silence. I've lost parts of myself trying to be accepted in systems that never saw me fully. I've denied my own vulnerability, swallowed my rage, and pushed through the pain just to make it to the next day. I've struggled with the "colonizer within" —that voice that whispers I'm not enough, not worthy, not lovable unless I erase myself. But I also know the sacredness of turning inward, of choosing to see those wounds and tend to them with compassion.

My healing began when I started to trust my own experience as wisdom. Not the voices of institutions or oppressors, but the truth my body carries—the truth my dreams whisper, my ancestors speak, and my community confirms. I've had to dig deep, to confront the ways I internalized lies and myths meant to keep me small. I've had to say no to invisibility, no to pretending, and yes to reclaiming my agency and identity. I have begun to see myself as a subject of my own history—not just a victim of it. I am learning to reclaim the parts of myself that were amputated, silenced, or shamed. I am no longer afraid to say I have needs. I am no longer ashamed to show my softness. And I am remembering how to feel—how to fully feel—not just pain, but joy, grief, tenderness, rage, and desire.

The Sacred Feminine calls me back to myself. I see her in the Black Mother who holds both joy and sorrow in her eyes. I meet her in the dark feminine, the part of me that was banished, feared, but who knows how to birth new worlds. I recognize her in the moments when I show up for my children and for myself, when I say, this is who I am, even when the world resists me. I've learned that healing also means reimagining the story. I rewrite the narrative of who I am and where I come from—sometimes through writing, memory, art, or the simple act of speaking truth. I honor the mestiza consciousness inside me, forged at the intersection of worlds, identities, and struggles. This consciousness is whole, even in its contradictions. It's a medicine that heals the split.

I've found strength in solidarity—linking arms with other women who know what it means to hurt, to rise, to resist. We gather in circles. We weep and rage and laugh together. We reclaim what was stolen. We build what we need. We practice transformative justice and center our communities around care, humanity, and liberation. And yes, motherhood has changed me too. It has stripped away illusions and required me to meet myself honestly. To raise children in this world while healing myself is a sacred task. It's not about perfection; it's about presence. Each day is an invitation to descend to my source and return a little more whole. Wholeness, for me, isn't about erasing pain—it's about transforming it. My wounds don't disappear, but they become sacred ground. They become stories. They become the soil where something new can grow. Healing is lifelong. It's cyclical. And it demands truth, community, reflection, and love. This journey is mine, but it's also ours. And we are not alone. We are many. And we are remembering. We are rising. We are becoming whole.

Chapter Eleven

DECOLONIZING THE FEMININE

For me, decolonizing the feminine has been a long, layered process—one that requires me to understand, confront, and begin to dismantle the ways my identity as a woman of color has been shaped, distorted, and repressed by colonialism and patriarchy. This journey isn't just personal. It's a collective unraveling—deeply tied to the stories of my ancestors, to the systems that raised me, and to the myths I've internalized about what it means to be feminine.

Colonial and Patriarchal Imposition – What I Inherited

I've come to see how colonialism and patriarchy have tried to script my womanhood. I was born into a world where white, Western ideals of femininity were positioned as the ideal—soft-spoken, pure, valuable only in proximity to whiteness. Everything about my body, my instincts, my ancestry was marked as "other," uncivilized, or dangerous. I've read the stories and I've felt the echoes in my bones: women like me were gagged, caged, bound into servitude, sterilized, and brutalized—our voices stolen, our bodies policed. I have witnessed how Women of Color have Theopoetically been flattened into one-dimensional figures—"strong," "resilient," or worse, "exotic," "primitive," or "victim." These monolithic images erased the complexity and power within us. They erased me. They taught me to fear the dark feminine—the instinctual, earth-rooted, emotional wisdom within—and instead taught me to chase safety in silence, control, and assimilation.

The Work of Decolonizing – What I'm Learning to Release and Reclaim

Decolonizing my feminine self means actively withdrawing my consent from the lies I inherited. It's about refusing the myths that have ruled my mind, my body, and my worth. I've had to do the hard, painful work of confronting the oppressor within—the part of me that still believes I need to shrink, obey, or earn my right to take up space. I've had to reclaim my own hands, my inner voice, my creative power. I've had to redefine who I am—not according to someone else's categories, but through the truth of my lived experience. This reclamation has taught me that identity isn't fixed—it's fluid, formed through pain, survival, joy, and relationship. I've begun to write new stories for myself. I've learned that my voice, my memory, my storytelling, are sacred tools. Tools for healing. Tools for resistance. I've also been remembering the sacred feminine that colonialism tried to erase—the wild, mysterious, intuitive force in me that connects me to earth, to dreams, to Spirit. Whether through the image of the Sacred Black Feminine or Sophia, I am learning to trust the feminine that lives in shadows and doesn't apologize for her depth or power.

This Isn't Just About Me – It's Collective

Decolonizing the feminine isn't a solo act. I walk this path with other Women of Color who are reclaiming their stories, challenging whitewashed feminism, and naming what's been stolen from us. We are building something new—together. We are creating spaces where our pain and our power can coexist, where our truths aren't filtered through a white gaze. We are writing ourselves back into history—not as footnotes, but as authors of a future where our wisdom is no longer silenced.

Major Ways Colonial Narratives Affect Self-Perception, Relationships, and Spirituality

1. Racial Hierarchies and Anti-Blackness in Self-Perception

Colonialism imposed a rigid racial hierarchy that placed European features and whiteness at the top while devaluing Blackness, leading to deeply ingrained anti-Black sentiments. For many Dominican women, this manifests as:

Colorism and Beauty Standards: Eurocentric beauty standards prioritize light skin, straight hair, and European facial features, making many women feel the need to alter their natural appearances through hair straightening, skin-lightening products, or aesthetic surgeries to conform to these ideals.

Internalized Anti-Blackness: Due to the colonial legacy of equating Blackness with inferiority, many Dominican women may struggle with fully embracing their African ancestry. This is compounded by the historical erasure of Black Dominican identity and the national emphasis on Hispanic heritage over African roots.

Identity Conflicts: Many Dominican women grow up hearing conflicting narratives about their racial and cultural identity, especially in relation to Haiti, due to the long-standing Dominican-Haitian divide reinforced by colonial and post-colonial governments.

2. Gender Roles and Marianismo in Relationships

Colonial Catholicism reinforced Marianismo, an ideology that idealizes women as pure, submissive, and self-sacrificing, mirroring the Virgin Mary. This belief system affects:
Romantic Relationships: Women are often socialized to prioritize male desires and needs, leading to patterns of emo-

tional labor, endurance of toxic relationships, and struggles with asserting personal agency.

Family Expectations: There is an expectation that Dominican women should be nurturing caregivers, often placing family responsibilities above their personal aspirations. Many women experience guilt when prioritizing their education or career over traditional roles.

Sexuality and Shame: Sexuality is often policed through a Catholic moral framework, leading to stigma around female sexual autonomy, double standards in gender expectations, and a culture of silence around sexual violence.
3. Catholicism and the Erasure of Afro-Indigenous Spirituality
Spanish colonial rule-imposed Catholicism as the dominant religion, forcefully converting the indigenous Taíno and enslaved Africans. This led to:

Suppression of Afro-Spirituality: African-based spiritual practices such as Santería, Vodou, and 21 Divisiones (Dominican Vodou) were demonized and forced underground. Many Dominican women who feel drawn to these traditions struggle with reconciling their spirituality with the stigma attached to them.

Religious Guilt and Fear: Many are taught that stepping outside of Catholic doctrine leads to spiritual condemnation, creating a fear-based relationship with faith and preventing some from exploring their ancestral spiritual practices.
Spiritual Double-Consciousness: Many Dominican women incorporate both Catholic practices and ancestral rituals into their spirituality but may feel internal conflict due to colonial indoctrination that labels African-based religions as "witchcraft" or "paganism."

Minor Yet Significant Ways Colonial Narratives Persist

1. Language and Cultural Inferiority

Many Dominican women are discouraged from speaking in Dominican Spanish dialects that include African linguistic influences, as they are often deemed "less refined" than standard Spanish. Colonial narratives suggest that speaking "proper Spanish" aligns with being educated and respectable, reinforcing class divides.

2. Preference for Europeanized Names and Norms

Names with African or Indigenous roots are often avoided in favor of Spanish or European names, reinforcing colonial preferences. Certain Dominican women face criticism for embracing natural hairstyles or wearing traditional African-inspired attire, as these styles have historically been stigmatized.

3. Sexuality and the Policing of the Feminine Body

Dominican women, especially those with curvier body types, often experience hyper-sexualization due to colonial-era fetishization of Black and mixed-race women. The virgin-whore dichotomy, inherited from Catholic colonial morality, still influences how women's bodies are perceived in relation to respectability.

4. Nationalism and the Haitian-Dominican Divide

Colonial-era anti-Haitian sentiment, later reinforced by Trujillo's dictatorship, still affects how Dominican women engage with racial identity and regional solidarity. Many Dominican women are taught to dissociate from African identity to distinguish themselves from Haitians, perpetuating racial divides that stem from colonial power structures.

A Wounded Mother

Reclaiming and Decolonizing the Feminine

While these narratives have deeply affected Dominican women's self-perception, relationships, and spirituality, there is an increasing movement toward reclaiming ancestral knowledge, redefining beauty and gender roles, and reconnecting with pre-colonial spiritual practices. Women are embracing natural Black and Afro-Taíno aesthetics as part of self-love. Rejecting toxic gender norms and advocating for feminist and Afro-Caribbean-centered perspectives. Reclaiming spiritual traditions like 21 Divisiones and honoring their African and indigenous ancestry. By critically engaging with and challenging these colonial narratives, Dominican women can forge paths toward self-acceptance, liberation, and empowerment—honoring both their wounds and their wisdom.

To heal, one must decolonize. This chapter unpacked how deeply embedded colonial narratives have affected self-perception, relationships, and spirituality. It examines how indigenous, African, and diasporic feminine traditions were suppressed, and how reclaiming these traditions can serve as a radical act of healing. Through an intersectional lens, it encourages readers to reimagine feminine power beyond white, patriarchal definitions—embracing a vision of the feminine that is fluid, self-determined, and deeply rooted in ancestral wisdom. By exploring thinkers, activists, and spiritual leaders who have worked to decolonize the feminine, this chapter provides readers with alternative frameworks for understanding and embodying their own power. It encourages an active dismantling of the narratives that have kept Women of Color in cycles of subjugation while offering pathways to spiritual and psychological liberation.

Chapter Twelve

A SACRED VULNERBILITY

Sacred Vulnerability, for me as a woman of color, is an intentional act—an act of reclaiming what has too often been used against me. I no longer see vulnerability as a weakness, but as a sacred source of power, wisdom, and liberation. For so long, my relationship to vulnerability was shaped by ancestral wounds and the systems that oppressed my people. But now, I am learning to see it differently. Growing up under the weight of patriarchal and Eurocentric ideals, I was taught that vulnerability made me a target—that my needs, emotions, and fears were liabilities. The legacy of colonialism, displacement, and racialized violence made vulnerability dangerous, not only for me but for the women who came before me. I saw what happened to those who dared to be soft: they were punished, silenced, or simply not believed. In this world, to need is to risk being met with disgust or dismissal—especially if you're a Black girl. I felt the pressure to perform strength, to live up to the "Strong Black Woman" identity that left no room for weakness or sorrow. That strength may have helped me survive, but it also cost me parts of myself. It quieted my humanity. But Sacred Vulnerability asks something different of me. It calls me to be real. It calls me to show up—not as the polished version the world wants, but as the whole woman I am, with all my messy, loud, tender parts. This is not just healing work; this is holy work.

For me, the Sacred Feminine—especially the Sacred Black Feminine and the archetype of Sophia—welcomes every part of my being. She embraces my neediness, my fear, my exhaustion. She doesn't ask me to be perfect. She says, "Come as you are." I turn to her when I feel broken, when I feel lost. I trust that she understands. After all, she, too, has been stolen. She, too, knows what it means to lose a child or to be cast out. With her, I don't have to pretend. With her, I am not too much. When I allow myself to fully feel—even the despair I was told to push away—I find something unexpected: wisdom. Somewhere in the pit of my gut, in that "terror in the gut," I hear a deeper voice guiding me toward healing. It's strange how surrendering to the pain can bring me closer to love. This isn't just about self-care; this is about spiritual transformation. This is about being able to feel again, to dream again, to believe that I am more than what they tried to make me. To walk this path, I have had to confront what I've internalized—the "oppressor within" that tells me to stay small, to be quiet, to earn my worth. I've had to let go of false selves I wore for survival. I've had to leave relationships that couldn't hold my truth. But in doing so, I've come back to myself. I've learned that vulnerability is where my true self lives. It's in the parts I once tried to hide that I find my power.

Strength, I now see, doesn't mean having it all together. It's the ability to stand in the gray areas, to admit that I'm afraid, to keep going anyway. Strength is surrender. It's trusting the deeper Self to carry me when my ego can't. That kind of strength doesn't puff up; it grounds me. Archetypes like Sophia remind me that even in suffering, there are treasures to be found. I am learning that I don't have to walk this road alone. When I surround myself with other Women of Color—those who are also learning to speak their needs and hold space for mine—I feel safer. In these matriarchal circles, need is not shameful; it's sacred. We build solidarity not just by speaking truth to power, but by telling the truth to ourselves and each other. In community, our vulnerability is met with empathy, and that changes everything.

In a world that teaches me to stay silent and self-sufficient, simply feeling becomes an act of rebellion. Letting my vulnerability show, naming my needs without apology, and refusing to disown my humanity is resistance. Honoring the unapologetic Blackness of the Sacred Feminine—something this world has tried to erase—is how I reclaim what's been stolen. So this is what Sacred Vulnerability means to me: it's the choice to be fully human, to show up whole, even when the world says I shouldn't. It's a path that asks everything of me—and in return, gives me back to myself. It's healing. It's truth. And it's liberation, not just for me, but for all of us.

CONCLUSION: BECOMING A WOUNDED MOTHER

Becoming a Wounded Mother has been, for me, a deeply transformative and often painful psychological journey—one that speaks not only to my personal experience, but also to the broader truth of what it means to be feminine, human, and whole. This path hasn't been linear or clean. It's been a spiral descent into myself: through pain, through self-exploration, and finally, toward a kind of reclamation.

The Wounded Part of Me

To be honest, I've come to see that to be human is to be wounded. My life story, like so many others, has grown around those wounds. Motherhood—or even the idea of it—has stirred up these old injuries, surfacing memories and emotions I thought I had long buried. Shame, doubt, self-hatred, despair, and disconnection are no strangers to me; they have all arrived like uninvited guests, asking to be seen and heard. At times, mothering has reawakened deep feelings of abandonment—especially the ache of having been "unmothered" myself. Facing the "oppressor within"—the internalized messages and identities I've clung to for survival—has been excruciating. But I've learned that healing cannot happen without first touching the wound. This truth echoes the archetype of the Wounded Healer, reminding me that my own pain, when embraced and transformed, becomes a source of medicine—not just for others, but for myself. Through the archetype of Sophia, who suffers, loves, and carries wisdom born of exile and endurance, I've found a spiritual companion. Her wounds mirror my own, and her resilience reminds me that divinity can be found in our most broken places.

The Mother I Am (and Am Becoming)

Motherhood, whether lived physically, symbolically, or spiritually, has been an alchemical fire for me. It has melted away old versions of myself, burning off illusions and reshaping my identity from the inside out. It's been a crucible, a sacred descent—like the goddesses of old who journeyed into the underworld, only to return transformed. Within this descent, I've had to confront the many faces of the Mother archetype—not just the nurturing presence, but the Dark Mother too. She has taught me magic, destruction, instinct, death, and rebirth. She has pulled me into the shadows of my own psyche, asking me to meet the fears I've tried to deny. Through this descent, I've had to surrender: to what I couldn't control, to the messiness of loving imperfectly, and to the unpredictability of my own emotions and instincts. This journey has forced me to differentiate between what I truly need and what the world has told me I should want. It has pushed me to listen—deeply—to the quiet wisdom within.

The Becoming

To become the Wounded Mother is to die to who I once was. It's to let go of comfort, to be defeated by the illusion of perfection, and to choose wholeness instead. It's in the mess, in the things I used to hide or push away, that I've discovered the parts of myself that are most vital. Reclaiming those pieces—my sensitivity, my rage, my unmet needs—has been the work of healing. I've stopped striving for perfection. Instead, I've chosen imperfect wholeness. I've allowed the opposites in me—light and dark, nurture and rage, hope and despair—to sit at the same table. And in doing so, I've discovered a deeper sense of meaning and purpose. This path is not about having it all together. It's about integration. About reclaiming wounded agency, reconnecting with buried instincts, and trusting that there is wisdom even in what feels broken. The journey isn't easy, but it is sacred. And it is mine. Becoming the Wounded Mother has taught me that suffering, when held with love and curiosity, can become the doorway to liberation. Through this archetypal unfolding, I have come home to myself—not perfect, but whole... Authentically me and not what others want me to be.

Chapter Thirteen

ANNOTATED BIBLIOGRAPHY

Abrams, Jeremiah, and Connie Zweig. Meeting the Shadow: The Hidden Power of the Dark Side of Human Nature. NY: J.P. Tarcher, 1991.
This book is crucial for understanding the "Wounded Mother" because it delves into the concept of the Shadow, a Jungian term for the unconscious aspects of the personality that are repressed or denied. The "Wounded Mother" archetype often carries deep wounds and traumas that become part of her Shadow. Exploring this Shadow is essential for her journey of self-love, as it involves acknowledging, integrating, and healing these hidden parts.

Anzaldúa, Gloria. Borderlands / La Frontera: The New Mestiza. San Francisco: Aunt Lute Books, 1999.
Anzaldúa's work is important because it brings a cultural and feminist perspective to the "Wounded Mother" archetype, particularly for those who exist in liminal spaces or at the intersection of multiple identities. Her concept of the "new mestiza" offers a framework for understanding how the "Wounded Mother" can navigate these borderlands and integrate seemingly conflicting aspects of her identity to achieve wholeness and self-love.

Cannon, Katie G. Black Womanist Ethics. Eugene, OR.: Wipf & Stock, 2006.
Cannon's book is vital for understanding the ethical dimensions of the "Wounded Mother" archetype within the context of Black womanhood. It addresses the specific challenges and ethical considerations faced by Black mothers who have been wounded by systemic oppression, racism, and sexism. Her work provides a framework for mothers to reclaim their self-worth and practice self-love while navigating these complex ethical landscapes.

Cleveland, Christena. God Is a Black Woman. New York: Harperone, 2022.
This book offers a powerful lens through which to view the "Wounded Mother" archetype by exploring the divine feminine in Black spirituality. It challenges traditional patriarchal representations of the divine and provides a space for Black mothers to connect with a source of strength, resilience, and self-love rooted in their own cultural and spiritual heritage.

Corbett, Lionel. Psyche and the Sacred: Spirituality Beyond Religion. NY: Routledge, 2020.
Corbett's work is relevant as it explores the connection between the psyche and the sacred, offering a broader understanding of spirituality beyond traditional religious frameworks. This is important for the "Wounded Mother" archetype because her journey of self-love may involve reconnecting with her own sense of the sacred and finding spiritual meaning in her experiences, independent of conventional religious beliefs.

Douglas, Kelly Brown. BLACK CHRIST. 25th Anniversary. NY: Orbis Books, 2019.
This book provides a theological perspective on the experiences of Black women, which is essential for understanding the "Wounded Mother" archetype within this specific cultural and religious context. It offers a powerful image of Christ that resonates with the struggles and resilience of Black mothers, providing a source of strength and self-affirmation.

Douglas, Kelly Brown. Stand Your Ground: Black Bodies and the Justice of God. NY: Orbis Books, 2015.
This work directly addresses the impact of racial injustice on Black bodies and spirits. For the "Wounded Mother," this book provides a critical analysis of the societal wounds inflicted upon her and her community, which must be acknowl-

edged and addressed in her journey toward self-love.

Edinger, Edward F. Ego and Archetype: Individuation and the Religious Function of the Psyche. MA: Shambhala, 1992.
Edinger's book is a cornerstone for understanding the Jungian concepts of ego, archetype, and individuation, which are central to the "Wounded Mother's" journey. It provides a theoretical framework for her process of psychological growth and self-discovery, as she integrates her woundedness into a more complete and individuated sense of self.

Eliade, Mircea. The Sacred and the Profane: The Nature of Religion. Translated by Willard Ropes Trask. FL: Harcourt Brace Jovanovich Book, 1987.
Eliade's work explores the fundamental distinction between the sacred and the profane in human experience. This is relevant to the "Wounded Mother" archetype because her journey may involve finding sacredness in her own life and experiences, even within the context of her wounds. It can help her to reframe her narrative and discover sources of meaning and transcendence.

Eliade, Mircea. Images and Symbols: Studies in Religious Symbolism. NJ: Princeton University Press, 1991.
In this book, Eliade delves into the power of symbols and images in religious and spiritual traditions. For the "Wounded Mother," understanding these symbols can be crucial in making meaning of her experiences and finding pathways to healing and self-love through symbolic expression and interpretation.

Erikson, Erik H. Childhood and Society. W. W. Norton & Company, 1963.
Erikson's work on psychosocial development provides a valuable framework for understanding how early childhood ex-

periences shape an individual's identity and sense of self. For the "Wounded Mother," this book can offer insights into how her own childhood wounds may have impacted her ability to mother herself and her children, and how she can address these patterns in her journey of self-love.

Freire, Paulo. Pedagogy of the Oppressed. NY: Continuum International Publishing Group, 2011.

Freire's work on liberation pedagogy is relevant to the "Wounded Mother" archetype, particularly for those who have experienced oppression and marginalization. His ideas on critical consciousness and empowerment can guide these mothers in their journey of self-love, as they learn to challenge oppressive systems and reclaim their own agency.

Griffin, David Ray. Archetypal Process: Self and Divine in Whitehead, Jung, and Hillman. IL: Northwestern University Press, 1989.

Griffin's book explores the intersection of archetypal psychology and process theology, offering a unique perspective on the relationship between the self and the divine. This can be relevant to the "Wounded Mother's" journey as she seeks to integrate her experiences with her spiritual beliefs and find meaning in her connection to a higher power or a sense of the divine.

Harris, Melanie L. Ecowomanism: African American Women and Earth-Honoring Faiths. Maryknoll (NY): Orbis Books, 2017.

Harris's work connects the experiences of African American women with earth-centered spiritualities. For the "Wounded Mother" within this context, this book provides a framework for understanding her connection to nature, her role as a nurturer, and the importance of ecological justice in her journey of self-love and healing.

Isasi-Díaz, Ada María. En La Lucha: In the Struggle: Elaborating a Mujerista Theology. Minneapolis: Fortress, 2004.
Isasi-Díaz's development of Mujerista theology is essential for understanding the "Wounded Mother" archetype within the context of Latina/Hispanic women's experiences. Her work addresses the specific challenges and struggles faced by these mothers and provides a theological framework for their empowerment and self-love.

Jung, C. G. Aion: Researches into the Phenomenology of the Self. NJ: Princeton University Press, 1969.
This is a core Jungian text that delves into the concept of the Self, the ultimate goal of individuation. For the "Wounded Mother," this book provides essential insights into her journey of becoming whole and integrating her woundedness into a larger sense of Self.

Jung, C. G. Memories, Dreams, Reflections. Vintage, 2011.
Jung's autobiographical work offers a personal glimpse into his own journey of self-discovery and individuation. This can be inspiring and insightful for the "Wounded Mother" as she navigates her own path of self-love and healing.

Jung, C. G, and R. F. C. Hull. Symbols of Transformation: An Analysis of the Prelude to a Case of Schizophrenia. NJ: Princeton University Press, 1990.
This book explores the transformative power of symbols in the process of psychological change. For the "Wounded Mother," understanding the symbolic language of her own experiences can be a key to unlocking healing and self-love.

Jung, C. G., Sonu Shamdasani, and Richard Francis. The Undiscovered Self with Symbols and the Interpretation of Dreams. NJ: Princeton University Press, 2011.
This work by Jung emphasizes the importance of self-knowl-

edge and the role of symbols and dreams in understanding the unconscious. These tools are invaluable for the "Wounded Mother" in her journey of exploring her inner world and finding meaning in her experiences.

Jung, Carl G. The Archetypes and the Collective Unconscious. NJ: Princeton University Press, 1959.
This book is foundational to Jungian psychology and introduces the concept of archetypes, universal patterns of behavior and imagery that reside in the collective unconscious. Understanding archetypes, including those related to the mother, is crucial for the "Wounded Mother" to recognize the deeper patterns influencing her life and to navigate her journey of self-love.

Jung, Carl G., and Beatrice M. Hinkle. Psychology of the Unconscious. NY: Dover Publications, 2002.
This early work by Jung explores the dynamics of the unconscious mind. It's relevant to the "Wounded Mother" archetype as it provides a basis for understanding how repressed emotions and experiences can influence her behavior and well-being, and how accessing the unconscious is essential for healing.

Jung, Carl G., and Murray Stein. Jung on Evil. NJ: Princeton University Press, 1995.
This book delves into the complex issue of evil and its psychological significance. For the "Wounded Mother," this can be important in coming to terms with the darker aspects of her own experiences and the world around her, and in integrating these into her journey of self-love and acceptance.

Koltuv, Barbara Black. The Book of Lilith. FL: Nicolas-Hays, Inc., 1986.
Koltuv's book explores the myth of Lilith, a powerful and often

misunderstood figure in mythology. Lilith's story can resonate with the "Wounded Mother" archetype, particularly in addressing issues of female power, autonomy, and the rejection of societal expectations. It can empower her to reclaim her own strength and embrace self-love on her own terms.

Marchiano, Lisa. MOTHERHOOD: Facing and Finding Yourself. CO: Sounds True, 2021.
This book directly addresses the challenges and transformations of motherhood, a central aspect of the "Wounded Mother" archetype. It provides guidance and support for mothers in navigating the complexities of their role while also attending to their own needs and well-being, fostering self-love in the process.

Matthews, Caitlin. Sophia: Goddess of Wisdom, Bride of God. Quest Books, 2013.
Matthews's exploration of the goddess Sophia offers a powerful feminine archetype of wisdom and divine connection. For the "Wounded Mother," this book can provide a source of inspiration and guidance as she seeks to reclaim her own inner wisdom and connect with a sense of the divine feminine in her journey of self-love.

Neumann, Erich. The Fear of the Feminine and Other Essays on Feminine Psychology. NJ: Princeton University Press, 1994.
Neumann's work delves into the psychological and cultural factors that contribute to the devaluation and suppression of the feminine. This is highly relevant to the "Wounded Mother" archetype, as it helps to understand the societal and psychological forces that may have contributed to her wounding and that she must confront on her path to self-love.

Neumann, Erich, and Ralph Manheim. The Great Mother: An Analysis of the Archetype. NJ: Princeton University Press, 2015.
This seminal work by Neumann provides an in-depth exploration of the Great Mother archetype, a complex and multifaceted figure that encompasses both nurturing and destructive aspects. Understanding this archetype is crucial for the "Wounded Mother" as she navigates her own relationship to motherhood, femininity, and the powerful forces of creation and destruction within herself.

Nouwen, Henri J. M. The Wounded Healer. New York: Doubleday, 1979.
Nouwen's book explores the concept of the wounded healer, an individual who, through their own suffering, develops a unique capacity to help others. This is highly relevant to the "Wounded Mother" archetype, as her own wounds can become a source of strength and empathy in her journey of self-love and in her relationships with others.

Staples, Tim. Behold Your Mother. Catholic Answers Press, 2017.
This book offers a religious perspective on motherhood, which can be relevant for "Wounded Mothers" seeking to integrate their faith with their experiences. It may provide comfort, guidance, or a framework for understanding their role within a spiritual context.

Tedlock, Barbara. The Woman in the Shaman's Body: Reclaiming the Feminine in Religion and Medicine. NY: Bantam Books, 2006.
Tedlock's book explores the historical and contemporary role of women in shamanism and healing practices. This is relevant to the "Wounded Mother" archetype as it highlights the potential for women to reclaim their healing powers and

connect with ancient traditions of feminine wisdom in their journey of self-love.

Ulanov, Ann Belford. The Feminine in Jungian Psychology and in Christian Theology. IL: Northwestern University Press, 1971.
Ulanov's work bridges Jungian psychology and Christian theology to explore the feminine dimension of both. This is important for "Wounded Mothers" who seek to integrate their spiritual beliefs with their psychological understanding of themselves, particularly in relation to their femininity.

Van Der Kolk, Bessel. The Body Keeps the Score: Brain, Mind, and Body in the Healing of Trauma. NY: Penguin Books, 2015.
Van Der Kolk's book is essential for understanding the impact of trauma on the mind and body. Since the "Wounded Mother" archetype often involves experiences of trauma, this book provides critical insights into the healing process and the importance of addressing the physical and emotional effects of trauma in her journey of self-love.

Waldron, Aaron. A Strange Fruit: A Theopoetics of Slavery in Amerika. Lost Raven Studios, 2024.
Waldron's work uses theopoetics to explore the legacy of slavery. This is important for understanding the "Wounded Mother" archetype within the context of the historical trauma of slavery and its ongoing effects on Black mothers and their journey toward Self-love.

Waldron, Aaron, and Yesenia Fernández Waldron. Our Mothers: A Meta-Spiritual Analysis of the Many Who Have Mothered Me. Lost Raven Studios, 2025.
This book broadens the concept of mothering beyond the biological/gender definition and uses Theopoetics with astrology to form a meta-spiritual analysis of the mothers who

have mothered the authors. This is relevant to the "Wounded Mother" archetype because it acknowledges the diverse forms of identity, mothering and support that can contribute to an individual's healing and Self-love.

Webster, Bethany. Discovering the Inner Mother. HarperCollins, 2021.

Webster's book directly addresses the concept of the "Inner Mother," a psychological construct that represents the nurturing and self-caring aspects within an individual. This is highly relevant to the "Wounded Mother" archetype, as cultivating a loving Inner Mother is crucial for healing from past wounds and developing a strong foundation of self-love.

Chapter Fourteen

APPENDIX

Theopoetry

DESPIERTA MADRE MIA

Yesenia Fernández Waldron

Despierta madre mia, esa carita con ausencia de amor, que falta me haces.

Te veo en persona pero no te encuentro quizas, un dia te conocere, pero se que no te has perdonado.

Despierta madre mia, que lastima al saber que estas aqui pero no me conozes, quiero que sepas que te perdono igual que a mi padre y que los años aqui en el mundo puedean superar su niñez sin tener que justificar a los demas.

Despierta madre mia,
y no nieges tu dolor, que ya son tantos años que te escondes en tu sombra. Dejate ver! que se que debajo de los lujos tu vez como importancia solo es la falta de amor propio que has olvidado.

UNA TAZA DE CAFE

Yesenia Fernández Waldron

No importa la trayectoria del tiempo ni la falta de consentimiento a las figuras de poder.

Una taza de café

Trae los recuerdos de voces que me rodeaban desde niña.

Voces que invitaban al vecino a una galleta de Cristina o un pedacito de pan caliente.

Es como si el tiempo se colgaba en un lugar sobre una cima de esperanzas.

Es hay que descubrí que existe una comunión con mis antepasados.

Mi vida no a sido fácil ni la de mi vecino,
Pero aún existe un puente que nos une, y revela la consciencia que compartimos.

No importa la trayectoria del tiempo ni la falta de consentimiento a las figuras de poder.

Sin embargo, se reconoce la delicadez de tomar las cosas con calma y a la vez, reconocer que la desconexión aún no existe. Lo que queda es la gratitud de poder compartir el momento sólo con una taza de café.

MAMÁ LETICIA

Yesenia Fernández Waldron

I was captivated by her hidden truths and eloquent beauty. She was a portrait dancing in her shadows.

I hear the night sounds of distant cars on the highway & echoes of neighborly fire alarms.

I am more connected to you now than ever as I experience the touch and taste of a Cuban cigar.

We were distant in person, but under the stars I remember you in every pull & intrinsic smell of my cigar.

There were times you would make me glow with your chosen words of flair & admiration.

You saw something in me that I at the time could not put into seldom words.

I was called "figurín" as my small posture was the invitation to the exchange of smiles & butterflies in my tummy.

At the time I couldn't articulate myself, but I was fascinated by mamas living room: a forest of greenery & smoke emblems of the untold story she carried.

I was captivated by her hidden truths and eloquent beauty. She was a portrait dancing in her shadows.

Till this day I don't fully know who you were, but my eyes wondered what you were like in your child like days.

A Wounded Mother

Your gazes & smiling eyes memorized me: like staring off into the beautiful night sky.

I remember you sitting beside me, on your red couch covered in plastic, wearing your solid red robe with your newly polished red nails that held a moist cigar from your salivated dark red lips.

You were a mystery to my eyes but maybe now as I go through my journey, my eyes will smile with the same glare you once gave me.

The dent left in your couch will never be filled, only the untold stories have become our families legacy.

I May I be the first to finally free myself, to pass down a key of hope and may those enter into a space of mystery but also self acceptance.

Let it be known that You are a part of me and I will always hold you close, not only on this night, but I will cherish you forever.

Rest in Love Mamá.